Enrichment

Consultant and Author
Dr. Fong Ho Kheong

Author
Ang Kok Cheng

US Distributor

HOUGHTON MIFFLIN HARCOURT

Published by Marshall Cavendish Education
An imprint of Marshall Cavendish International (Singapore) Private Limited
Times Centre, 1 New Industrial Road, Singapore 536196
Customer Service Hotline: (65) 6411 0820
E-mail: tmesales@sg.marshallcavendish.com
Website: www.marshallcavendish.com/education

Distributed by
Houghton Mifflin Harcourt
222 Berkeley Street
Boston, MA 02116
Tel: 617-351-5000
Website: www.hmheducation.com/mathinfocus

First published 2009
2013 Edition

Math in Focus® Enrichment 4A
ISBN 978-0-669-01580-5

Printed in Singapore

4 5 6 7 8 1401 18 17 16 15 14 13
4500404079 A B C D E

Contents

CHAPTER 1 **Place Value of Whole Numbers** 1

CHAPTER 2 **Estimation and Number Theory** 8

CHAPTER 3 **Whole Number Multiplication and Division** 16

CHAPTER 4 **Tables and Line Graphs** 23

CHAPTER 5 **Data and Probability** 35

CHAPTER 6 **Fractions and Mixed Numbers** 45

Answers 54

Introducing

Math in Focus®

Enrichment

Written to complement *Math in Focus®: Singapore Math by Marshall Cavendish* Grade 4, exercises in *Enrichment 4A* and *4B* are designed for advanced students seeking a challenge beyond the exercises and questions in the Student Books and Workbooks.

These exercises require children to draw on their fundamental mathematical understanding as well as recently acquired concepts and skills, combining problem-solving strategies with critical thinking skills.

Critical thinking skills enhanced by working on *Enrichment* exercises include classifying, comparing, sequencing, analyzing parts and whole, identifying patterns and relationships, induction (from specific to general), deduction (from general to specific), and spatial visualization.

One set of problems is provided for each chapter, to be assigned after the chapter has been completed. *Enrichment* exercises can be assigned while other students are working on the Chapter Review/Test, or while the class is working on subsequent chapters.

Name: ______________________ Date: ______________

Place Value of Whole Numbers

Thinking Skills

Solve.

1. A thief left a secret code for the police at the scene of a crime. Use the clues to help the police solve the secret code.

- The number of legs a spider has is the same as the digit in the thousands place.
- The digit in the tens place is 2 less than the digit in the thousands place.
- The digit in the ones place is half the digit in the thousands place.
- The digit in the hundreds place is the same as the digit in the ones place.
- The digit in the ten thousands place is 3 more than the digit in the ones place.

Ten Thousands	Thousands	Hundreds	Tens	Ones

The secret code is ______________.

Name: ______________________ Date: ______________

Match the numbers with the correct cards. The first one has been done for you.

2. There are five number cards, A, B, C, D, and E, in a stack.
Each card has a number on the reverse side.

- The number on card A is the greatest number.
- Card B has the least number.
- The numbers on card C and card B have a difference of 7,161.
- The number on card D is greater than the number on card C but less than the number on card E.

______	______	A	______	______
41,584	**56,783**	**61,376**	**59,371**	**48,745**

Form the greatest possible 5-digit number using the clues.

3.
- All five digits are different.
- None of the five digits are 1.
- The digit in the ten thousands place is greater than 7.
- The sum of all five digits is 18.
- The greatest digit is equal to the sum of the other four digits.

Ten Thousands	Thousands	Hundreds	Tens	Ones

The number is ______________.

Name: ______________________ Date: ______________

Count back and fill in the blanks.

4. 12,250 11,000 ________ 8,500 7,250 ________

Answer the questions.

5. Kim makes a pattern using circles and squares joined together by lines. The first three designs she makes are shown. Find the rule that Kim is using to make the pattern.

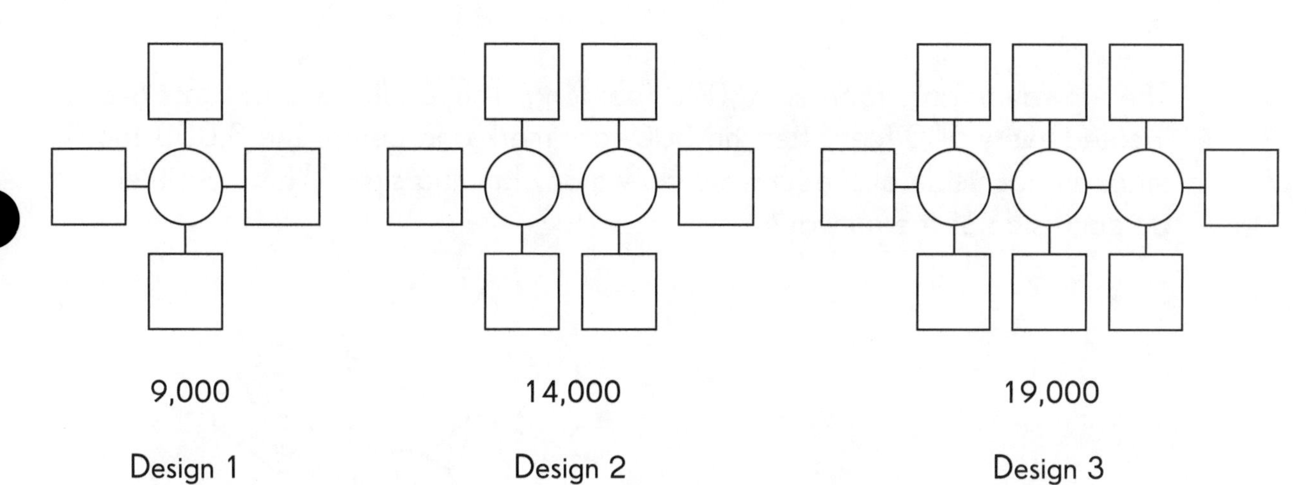

What is the number for Design 8? ____________

Name: ______________________ **Date:** ______________

6. Which number does not belong in the group? Color it. Explain your answer.

11,604	12,604	10,604
15,504	14,604	13,604

7. The runway of an airport is 10,000 feet long. The landing signal lights are located every 500 feet after the 500-foot mark and before the 8,000-foot mark on each side of the runway. How many landing signal lights are there on each side of the runway?

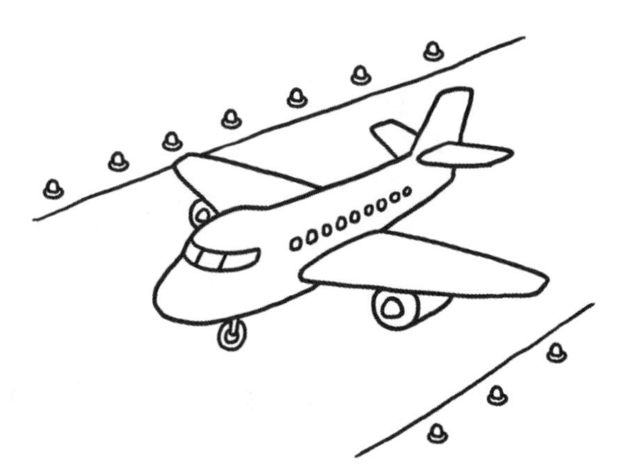

Name: ____________________ Date: ____________

Exploration

Use the digits to make 5-digit numbers.

7 0 2 9 6

8. Write the greatest possible 5-digit number. ____________

9. Write the least possible 5-digit number. ____________

10. The difference between the greatest possible number and the least possible number is ____________.

Solve.

11. A store earns $20,009 in year 1, $24,010 in year 2, and $28,011 in year 3. If this pattern continues, how much will the store earn in year 4? ____________

Write three 5-digit numbers to complete the pattern.

12. 47,296 45,236 ________ ________ ________

Name: ______________________ Date: ______________

Jerry compared these numbers and wrote the following statements. What mistakes did Jerry make?

76,218	56,218	14,573	24,573

13. 76,218 is 2,000 more than 56,218.

____

____

14. 24,573 is 10,000 less than 14,573.

____

____

Write a statement comparing these numbers.

15.

82,018	63,018	74,158

____

____

____

Name: ______________________ Date: ______________

Write the steps needed to order this set of numbers from least to greatest on the number line. Then write the numbers on the number line by following the steps.

16.

35,570	36,570	36,500	36,545	36,565

Step 1 ______________________

____

____

Step 2 ______________________

____

____

Step 3 ______________________

____

____

Name: ______________________ Date: ______________

Estimation and Number Theory

Thinking Skills

Solve. Show your work.

1. I am a factor of 50 and a multiple of 5.
I am a 2-digit number greater than 10 but less than 40.
What number am I?

2. Ms. Atkinson estimates a total cost of $90 for her grocery bill. If she rounds the cost of each item on her grocery bill to the nearest ten dollars, what is the least possible price Ms. Atkinson will pay for the fish?

Items	Cost ($)
Muffins	18
Milk	12
Meat	25
Fish	?

Name: ______________________ **Date:** ______________

Solve.

3. Find the sum of all the factors of 48 and the sum of all the factors of 64. Then find the difference between the two sums.

4. Two factors of 32 are x and y. The sum of x and y is 12. The smaller of the two numbers is x. Find the value of x and y.

Name: ______________________ **Date:** ______________

Strategies

Answer the questions.

5. Ms. Duff wants to give her students some apples.
If she gives each student 7 apples, there will be no apples left.
If she gives each student 4 apples, there will be 18 apples left.
How many students are in Ms. Duff's class?

6. Which number does not belong in the group? Color it.
Explain your answer.

72

54 24

18 49 36

27 15

Name: ______________________ Date: ______________

Solve.

7. These numbers are multiples of two numbers. Rewrite them into two sets of five multiples. Some numbers will be used in both sets of multiples.

64 16 27 18 24 48 9 32

Numbers	Multiples				

8. Ricky works part-time at a store every 2 days.
Anwar also works part-time at the same store every 3 days.
They first met at the store on a Monday.
On which day will they meet for

a. the second time?

b. the third time?

Name: ______________________ Date: ______________

Exploration

Solve.

9. Make a list of the first nine multiples of 9.
Then multiply 9 by consecutive whole numbers to show how to find the multiples. Lastly divide the multiples by the same consecutive whole numbers to get a quotient of 9.
The first one has been done for you.

Multiples of 9	Multiply	Divide
9	$1 \times 9 = 9$	$9 \div 1 = 9$

10. What do you notice in the second and third columns?

____

____

____

Name: _______________ Date: _______________

Answer the question.

11. Estimate the sum and the difference of 7,309 and 2,876 using two estimation methods. Which method gives you the more accurate answers?

Method 1

Method 2

Name: ______________________ Date: ______________

Solve.

12. Clark estimates the sum of two numbers using two methods.
Write the steps used in each method.
Name each method used.

a. Method 1 ______________________

4,728 + 1,095 = ?

Estimated sum is 5,000.

Step 1 ______________________

Step 2 ______________________

b. Method 2 ______________________

4,728 + 1,095 = ?

Estimated sum is 5,800.

Step 1 ______________________

Step 2 ______________________

Name: ______________________ Date: ______________

13. Jack, Keith, and Lee completed these estimation problems. Find the errors.

a. Estimate the product of 247 and 3 by rounding to the nearest hundred.

Jack $247 \times 3 = ?$
$300 \times 3 = 900$

Error: ______________________

____

b. Estimate the quotient of 95 and 4.

Keith $95 \div 4 = ?$
$80 \div 4 = 20$

Error: ______________________

____

c. Estimate the quotient of 73 and 3.

Lee $73 \div 3 = ?$
$90 \div 3 = 30$

Error: ______________________

____

Name: ______________________ Date: ______________

Whole Number Multiplication and Division

Thinking Skills

Answer the questions. Show your work.

1. The fifth multiple of a number is the quotient of 480 and 8.
What is the number?

2. Ms. Rodney bakes 1,102 cookies. She packs the cookies into small bags.
Each bag has 9 cookies. If 56 cookies are broken and discarded,
what is the least number of bags Ms. Rodney needs to pack
all the remaining cookies?

Name: ______________________ Date: ______________

3. A store manager ordered 28 crates of mangoes. There were 36 mangoes in each crate. When the mangoes were delivered, he sold the ripe mangoes and repacked the rest equally into 73 boxes. There were 12 mangoes in each box. How many ripe mangoes were sold?

Name: ______________________ Date: ______________

Answer the questions. Show your work.

4. Ms. Andrews distributed 1,000 pens among her students.
She put the remaining pens into 120 packets of 5 pens each.
How many pens did Ms. Andrews have at first?

5. I am a 4-digit number.
I am divisible by 6, but not by 9.
The product of my first two digits is 20, and the difference between my last two digits is 3.
All my digits add up to 24, and my digit with the least value is 4.
When my first and last digits are added, the sum is 11.
All my digits are different. What number am I?

1st digit	**2nd digit**	**3rd digit**	**4th digit**

6. Fill in the blanks. Use the least possible divisor.

______ ÷ ______ = 143 R 6

Name: ______________________ **Date:** ______________

7. Jared has some birds and dogs in his garden. He counts a total of 12 heads and 30 legs in all. How many birds and dogs are in Jared's garden?

8. Mr. Winters borrowed tables and chairs for a party.
The number of chairs borrowed by Mr. Winters is 3 times the number of tables. If there are 80 legs on the furniture altogether, how many tables and chairs did Mr. Winters borrow?

Name: ______________________ Date: ______________

PROBLEM SOLVING

Exploration

Answer the questions.

9. Write 8,216 in as many ways as possible.

Example

8,216 = 8 thousands 21 tens 6 ones

10. Write two division problems by using the words and numbers given below.

Mr. Jackson	children	child	$250	$1,250
how	much	money	divides	5

a. ____

____

b. ____

____

Name: ______________________ Date: ______________

Solve.

11. Write the steps you use to multiply 3,275 by 5.

Step 1 ______________________

____

Step 2 ______________________

____

Step 3 ______________________

____

Step 4 ______________________

____

12. Find the actual product.

$$\begin{array}{r} 3,275 \\ \times \quad 5 \\ \hline \end{array}$$

Name: ______________________ Date: ______________

Solve.

Kelvin and Melvin made mistakes while solving these problems.
Explain the mistakes they made.

13. Kelvin

$$\begin{array}{r} 4,075 \\ \times \quad 5 \\ \hline 2003525 \end{array}$$

____

____

14. Melvin $4,075 \div 5 = 8,105$

____

____

Write the steps used to estimate the product.

15. 827×53

Step 1 ____

Step 2 ____

Step 3 ____

Name: ______________________ Date: ______________

Tables and Line Graphs

Study the table and answer the questions.

Tacos Sold at a Food Court

Taco Filling	Quantity Sold	Total Sales
Chicken	42	$42
Beef	50	$100
Vegetarian	28	$28
Seafood	33	$66

1. Which type of taco filling was the most popular? ______________

2. Which type of taco filling had total sales of less than $30?

____

3. What is the cost of a beef taco? $______________

4. Which is more expensive, a chicken taco or a seafood taco? ______________

Name: ______________________ Date: ______________

Study the table and answer the questions.

The table shows the number of students who attended football practice during a week of bad weather.

Students at Football Practice

Day of the Week	Number of Students
Monday	15
Tuesday	25
Wednesday	10
Thursday	8
Friday	5

5. How many students in total were at football practice on Monday and Tuesday? ______________

6. How many more students were present on Tuesday than on Thursday? ______________

7. On which day did the greatest number of students miss football practice? ______________

8. Why do you think more students were absent on Friday than on Tuesday?

____

____

Name: ______________________ Date: ______________

Study the line graph and answer the questions.

An environmental group held a tree-planting event. The table shows the number of trees planted over the first five hours of the day.

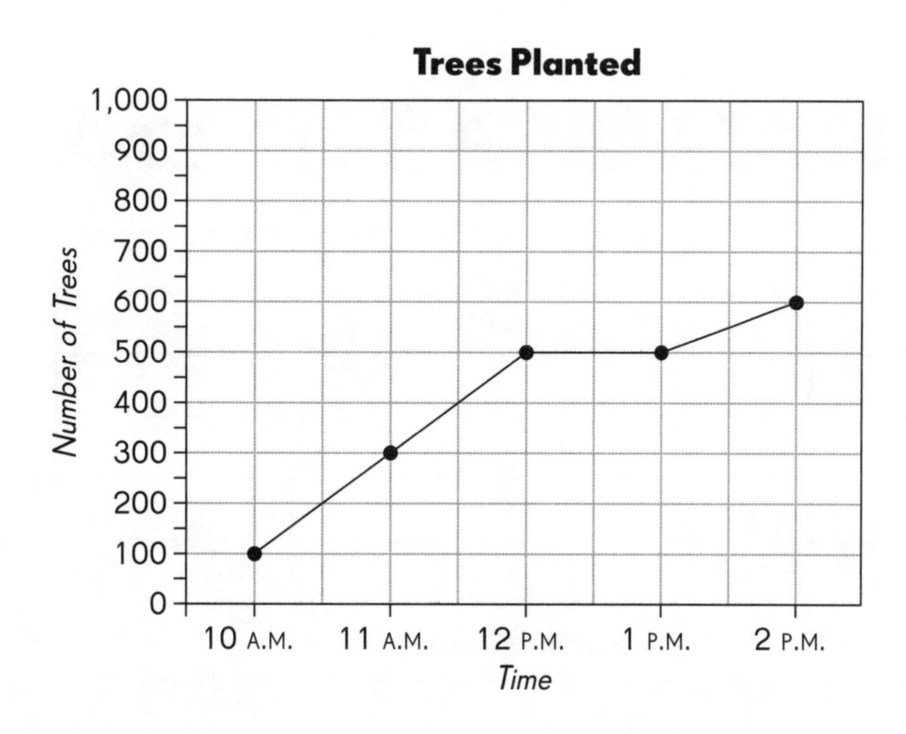

9. In which 1-hour interval was there no change in the number of trees planted?

____

10. If the group plants trees for another hour, is it likely that the total number of trees planted will be above 1,000? Why?

____

____

Name: ______________________ Date: ______________

Complete the table and the bar graph. Then answer the questions.

A total of 160 boxes were inspected for rotten oranges. The table and the bar graph show the number of rotten oranges found in each box.

11. **Rotten Oranges**

Number of Rotten Oranges	Number of Boxes
0	40
1	50
2	
3	
4	
5	10

12.

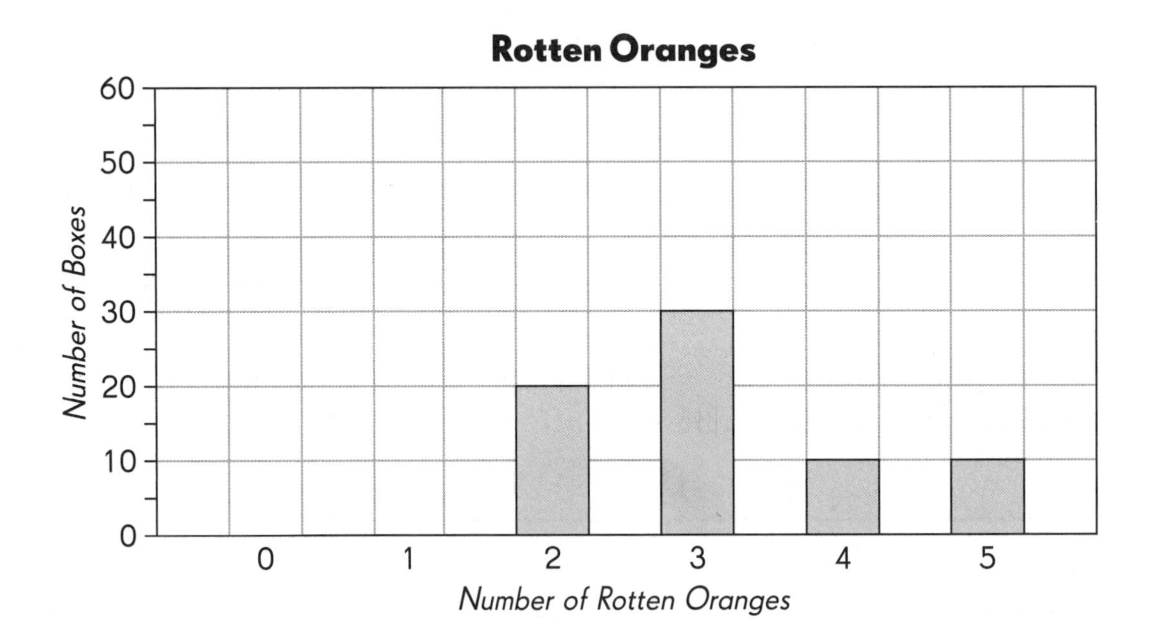

13. How many boxes contained more than 2 rotten oranges? ______________

14. How many rotten oranges were found altogether? ______________

Name: _______________ Date: _______________

Strategies

Answer the questions. Show your work.

The table shows the number of baseball cards three students have.

Students	Haley	Steve	Phoebe
Number of Cards	18	27	135

15. How many cards must Phoebe give Haley and Steve so that all three students have the same number of cards? _______________

____

At a barbeque, Justin grills some jalapenos. He gives Nathan 15 jalapenos and Austin 23 jalapenos. Justin now has 24 grilled jalapenos left. The number of jalapenos that each boy has is shown in the table.

Boys	Austin	Justin	Nathan
Number of Jalapenos	42	24	25

16. How many grilled jalapenos did Justin have at first? _______________

17. What was the total number of grilled jalapenos that Austin and Nathan had at first? _______________

Name: ____________________ Date: ____________

Study the graphs and answer the questions on the next page.

The graphs below show the results of two surveys on students' favorite sports. The surveys were conducted six months apart.

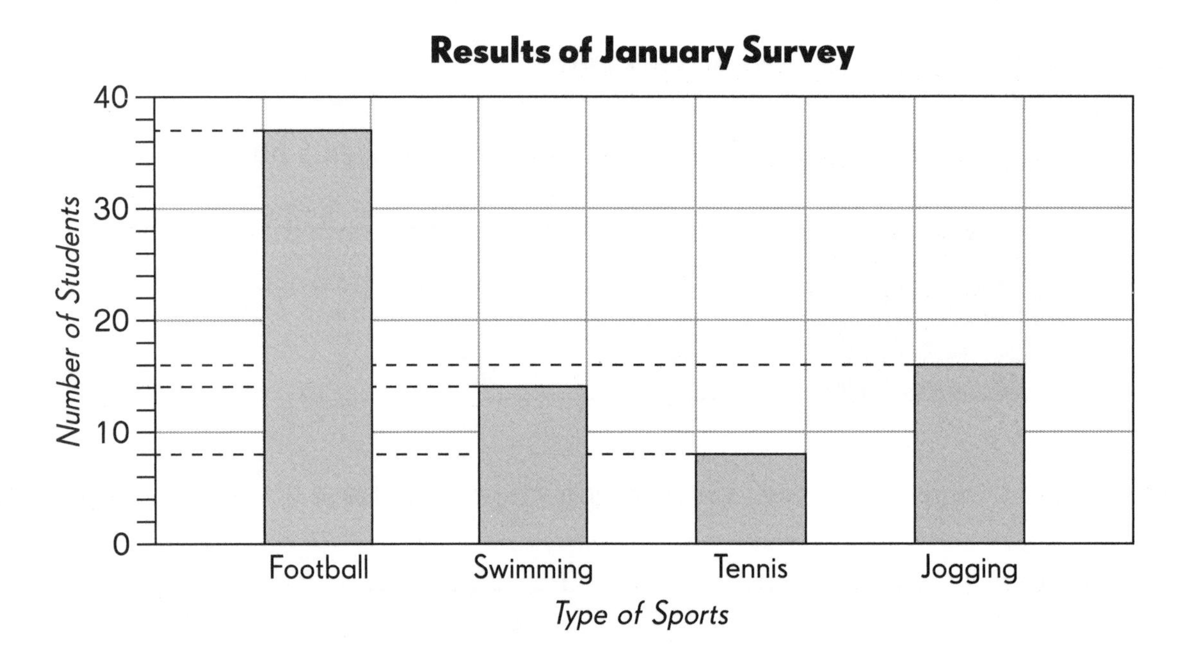

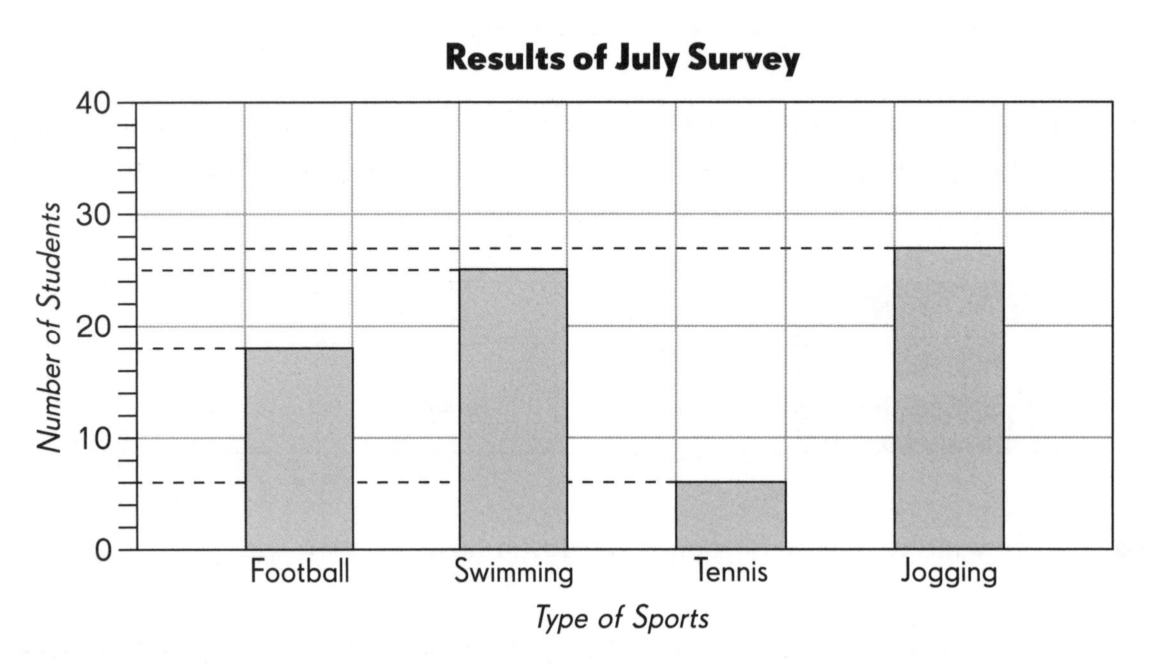

Name: ______________________ Date: ______________

18. How many more students chose jogging in July than in January?

____

19. How many more students chose football or jogging over swimming or tennis in January? ______________

20. Was there an increase or a decrease in the number of students who chose football or swimming in July than in January? How much was the increase or decrease? ______________________

21. What type of graph could have been used to show the change in the students' favorite sports from January to July? ______________

Name: ______________________ Date: ______________

Complete the graph.

22. The line graph shows the cost of a type of wire sold in a hardware store. Find the cost of the wire when the lengths are 30 meters and 35 meters. Show them on the graph.

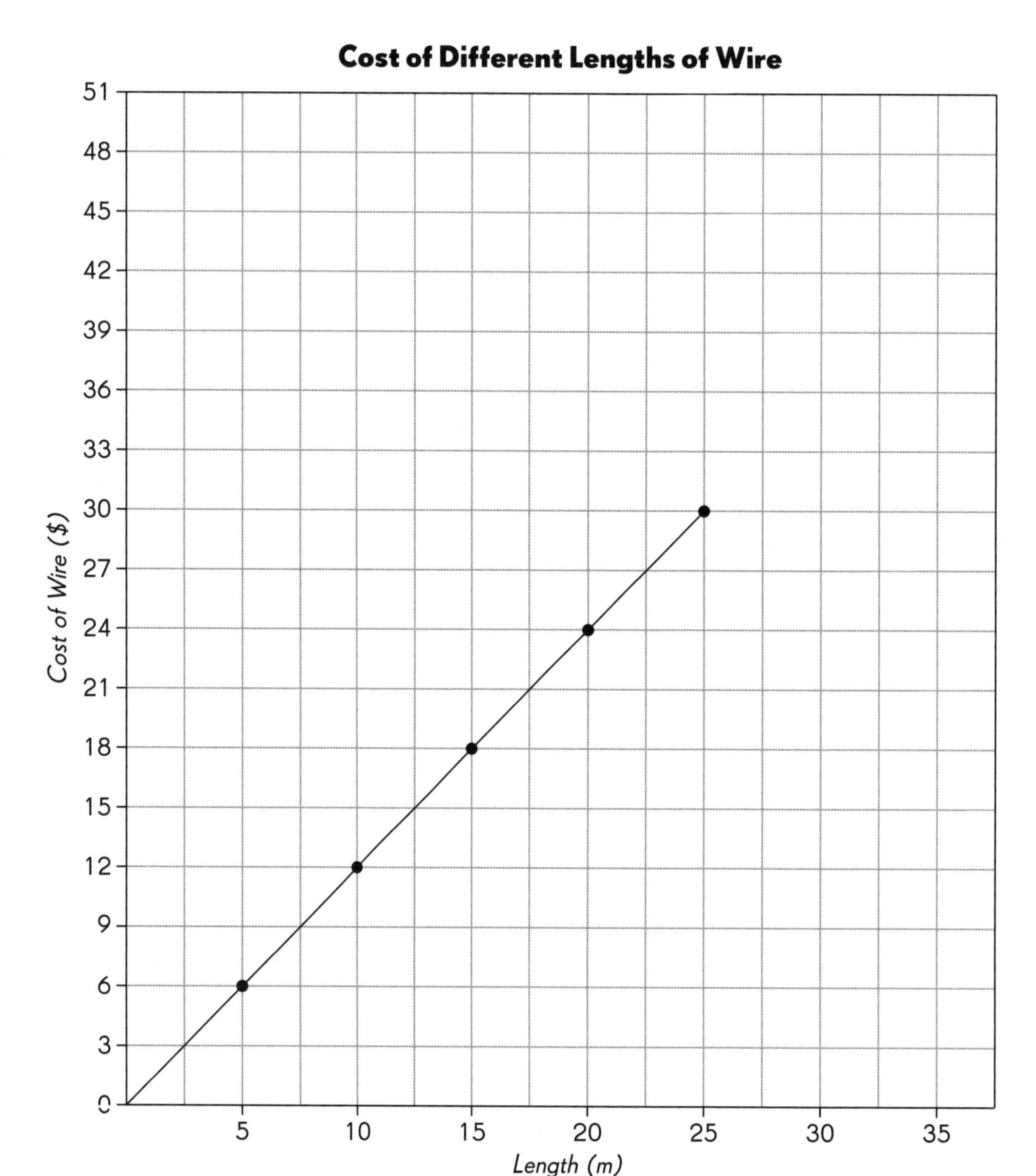

Name: ______________________ **Date:** ______________

Complete the line graph.

23. Below is an incomplete line graph. The temperature of the aquarium at 12 P.M. is missing. One possible temperature at this time is shown. Use different colors to show two other possible temperatures of the aquarium at 12 P.M.

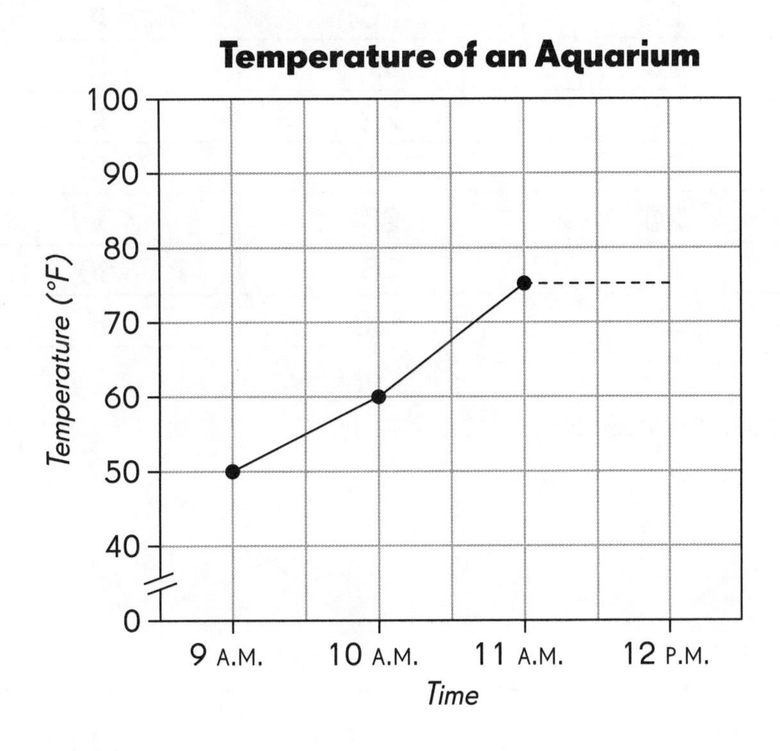

Give reasons to support your graphs. The first one has been done for you.

Case 1: The temperature of the aquarium at 12 P.M. is the same as its temperature at 11 A.M.

Case 2: ______________________________

Case 3: ______________________________

Name: ____________________ Date: ____________

Complete the table. Then draw a bar graph and a picture graph.

The table shows the total number of red and green apples in six different boxes. The table has some missing data.

Box	Number of Green Apples	Number of Red Apples	Total Number of Apples
1	25	20	**A**
2	24	**B**	45
3	23	22	**C**
4	20	**D**	45
5	25	20	**E**
6	**F**	25	50
Total	**G**	133	**H**

24. Show how you find the missing data.

Example

A = 25 + 20 = 45

B = ____________________

C = ____________________

D = ____________________

E = ____________________

F = ____________________

G = ____________________

H = ____________________

Name: ______________________ Date: ______________

25. Draw a bar graph to show the number of red apples in the six boxes.

26. Draw a picture graph to show the total number of apples in the six boxes.

Name: ______________________ Date: ______________

Write questions.

The line graph shows the number of visitors at a store over the first four hours of the day.

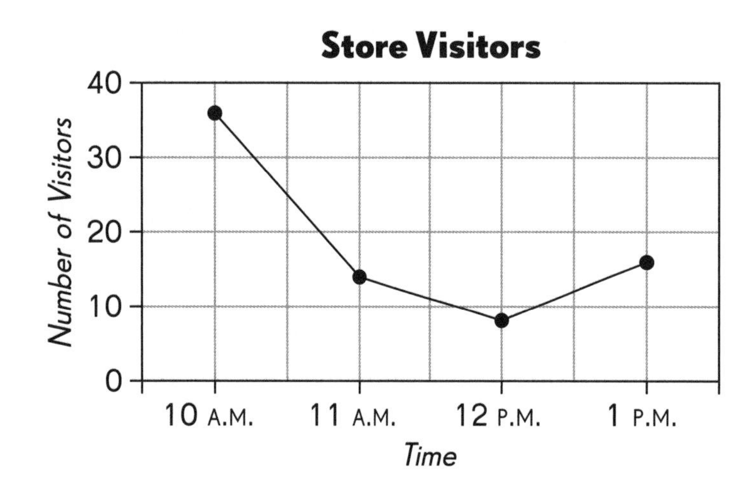

27. Write four questions based on the graph.
Use the words in the boxes to form your questions.

altogether	how	many	more than	less than
	more	why	fewer	

Question 1: ______________________

____

Question 2: ______________________

____

Question 3: ______________________

____

Question 4: ______________________

____

Name: ______________________ Date: ____________

Data and Probability

Thinking Skills

Answer each question. Show your work.

1. Allison's average score on four tests is 65.
If her lowest test score is left out, her average score for the three remaining tests would be 69. What is Allison's lowest score?

2. Jamal has a deck of 52 playing cards. What is the probability of drawing a 3, 4, or 5 of diamonds in a single draw? Write your answer as a fraction in simplest form.

3. The mean of this set of data is 55.
What is the value of x?

23 34 67 x 23 73 87

Name: ______________________ Date: ______________

Complete.

4. A school club wanted to sell flavored drinks to raise money for their activities. The club conducted a survey of 50 students to choose the flavors. The table shows the results of the survey.

Complete the table and help the club fill in their report using *impossible*, *certain*, *more likely*, or *less likely*.

Flavor	Number of Students	Likelihood of High Sales
Cherry	21	
Lime	9	
Grape	3	
Raspberry	17	
Orange	0	

Report:

We were ______________ that of the 50 students surveyed, no one liked orange-flavored drinks. It is ______________ that we are going to sell a lot of lime-flavored and grape-flavored drinks. Both the cherry and raspberry flavors are ______________ to sell very well. It would be ______________ to sell orange-flavored drinks to the students surveyed.

Name: ______________________ Date: ______________

Solve.

The stem-and-leaf plot shows the weights of 15 crates of oranges and apples. The part of the plot showing the weights of the two heaviest crates was torn away.

Weights of Crates (pounds)

Stem	Leaves
1	9
2	0 3 3 4 8
3	1 4 5 5 5
4	0 1

1 | 9 = 19

5. The mode of the set of data is __________ pounds.

6. The average weight of the four heaviest crates is 41 pounds. Find the range of the crate weights.

Name: ______________________ Date: ______________

Answer the questions.

7. There are five prize coupons for 2 baseball gloves, 2 baseball caps, and 1 baseball bat in a bag. Austin picks out a coupon from the bag. What is the probability that Austin will win a baseball cap?

8. Shayla has 28 balls of yarn in a box. Twelve balls of yarn are red, two are purple, eight are blue, and the rest are white. She decides to pull a ball of yarn randomly from the box. Is it more likely that Shayla will pull out a red ball of yarn than a blue or white ball of yarn?

Name: ______________________ **Date:** ______________

Solve. Show your work.

9. A mystery set of 5 numbers has a mean of 24, a median of 18, and a range of 42. The second greatest number is 36 and the least number is 6. List all the 5 numbers from the least to the greatest.

______ ______ ______ ______ ______

least greatest

Name: ____________________ Date: ____________________

10. There are seven cards labeled with the numbers 1 through 7.

1	2	3	4	5	6	7

a. Find the median of this set of cards.

b. Four cards are selected at random from these seven cards. The four cards selected have an average greater than the median of the seven original cards. Make a list of all possible combinations of the four random cards selected.

Name: ________________________ Date: ____________

Exploration

Solve.

11. You are given 5 bags, 10 red balls, and 10 green balls. Describe how you would distribute the balls in each bag so that the likelihood of drawing a green ball from any bag is

a. equally likely as drawing a red ball

b. impossible

c. certain

d. more likely than drawing a red ball

e. less likely than drawing a red ball

Name: ______________________ Date: ______________

Solve.

12. Kathy made a spinner with 16 equal parts. She colored the parts yellow, green, and blue. When the spinner is spun, the probability of landing on yellow is $\frac{3}{16}$. The probability of landing on green is greater than the probability of landing on yellow but less than the probability of landing on blue. Color the spinner. There is more than one solution.

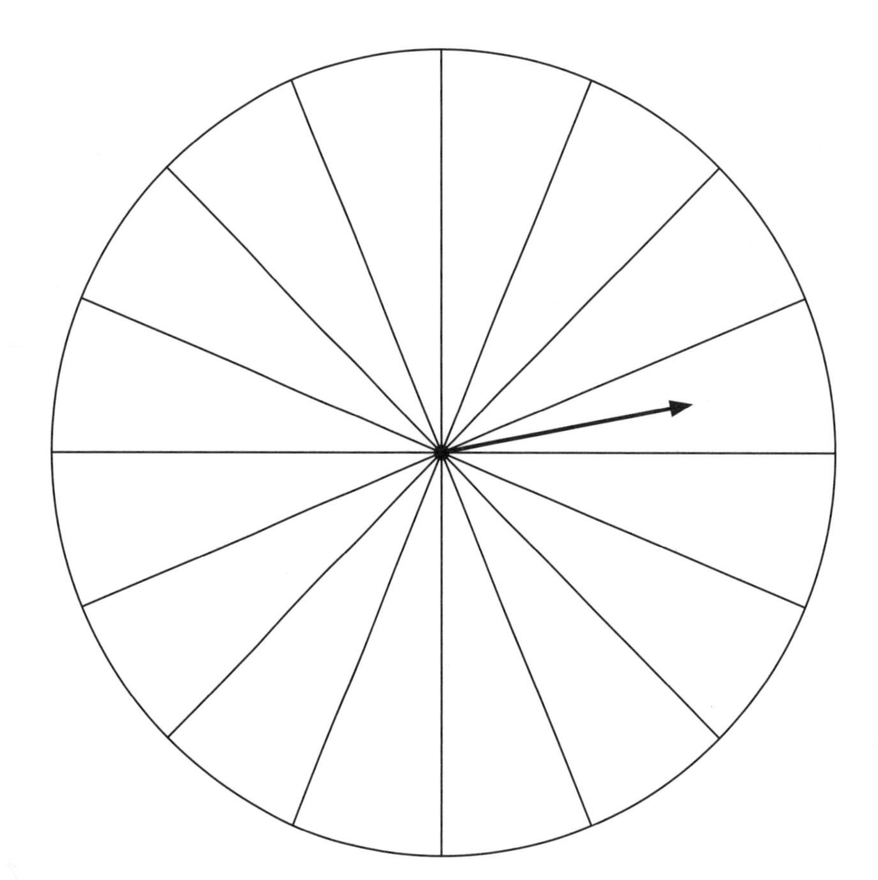

Name: ____________________ Date: ____________

Write real-world problems.

13. 57 | 70 | 56 | 77

Use the data set to write a real-world problem using the word *mean*.

14. 183 | 257 | 269 | 350 | 410 | 436 | 475 | ?

An unknown number is added to the data set. Write a real-world problem that requires the following steps for the solution.

$183 + 257 + 269 + 350 + 410 + 436 + 475 = 2{,}380$

$2{,}496 - 2{,}380 = 116$

Name: ______________________ Date: ______________

Explain.

15. A number cube has six faces numbered 1 through 6. The line plot shows how many times each number occurred when the number cube was tossed. Each ✗ represents one occurrence. Explain how to find the mean, median, and mode from the line plot.

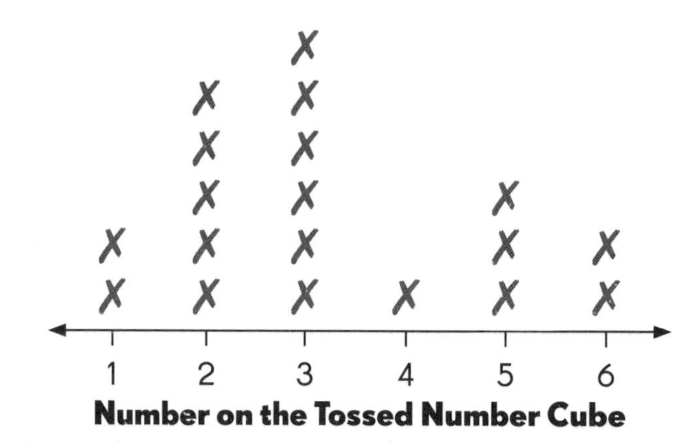

Mean:

____

____

Median:

____

____

Mode:

____

____

Name: ______________________ Date: ______________

Fractions and Mixed Numbers

Solve.

1. The figure is a square divided into many smaller pieces. What fraction of the square is the rectangle?

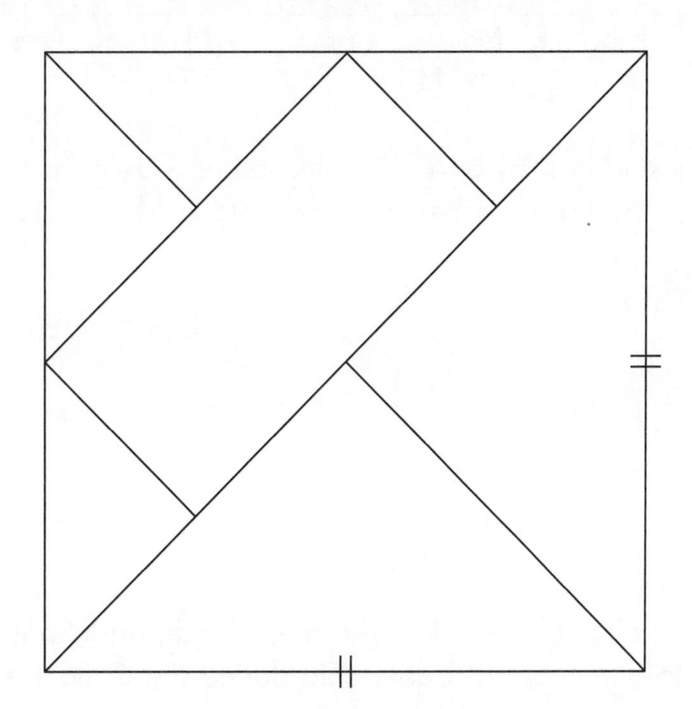

Name: ______________________ Date: ______________

Use the graph. Express the answers in simplest form.

2. The graph shows the number of books sold by Mr. Harrods for the last 6 months.

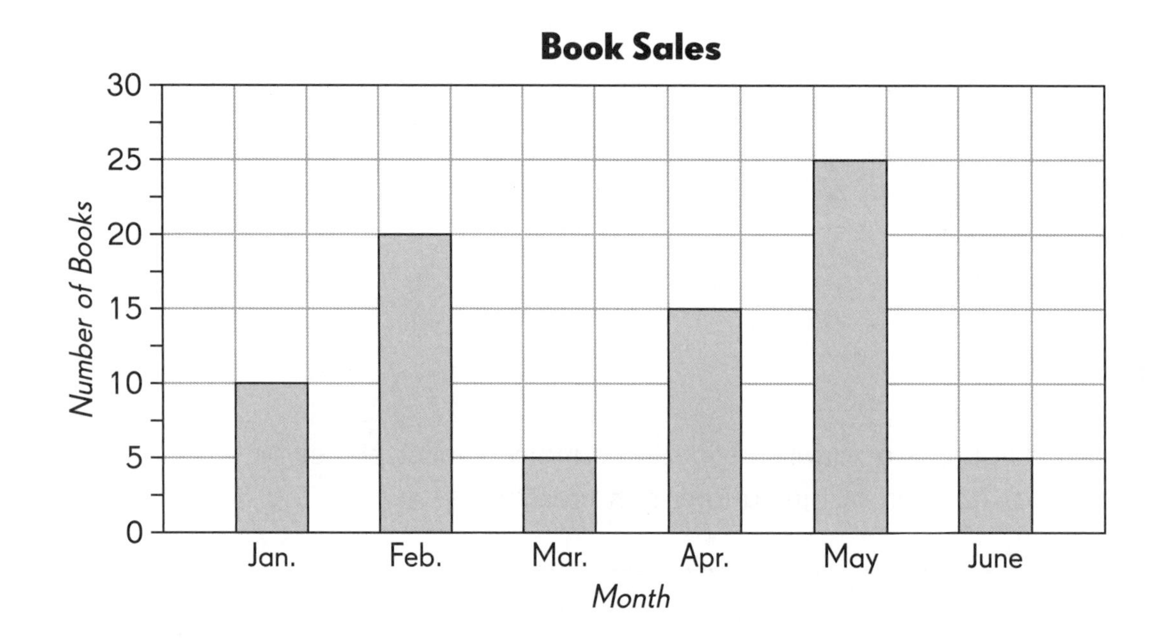

a. 14 of the books sold in May and June altogether were comic books. What fraction of the total number of books sold in May and June were comic books?

b. Write the number of books sold in February, March, and April as a fraction of the total number of books sold during the 6 months.

Name: ______________________ **Date:** ______________

Answer the questions. Express answers in simplest form.

3. Raj poured $4\frac{2}{3}$ liters of water equally into identical cups.
Each cup contained $\frac{2}{9}$ liter of water.
How many cups did Raj use?

4. In the figure, X and Y are identical overlapping squares. If the length of each side of the shaded region is half the length of square X, what fraction of the figure is not shaded?

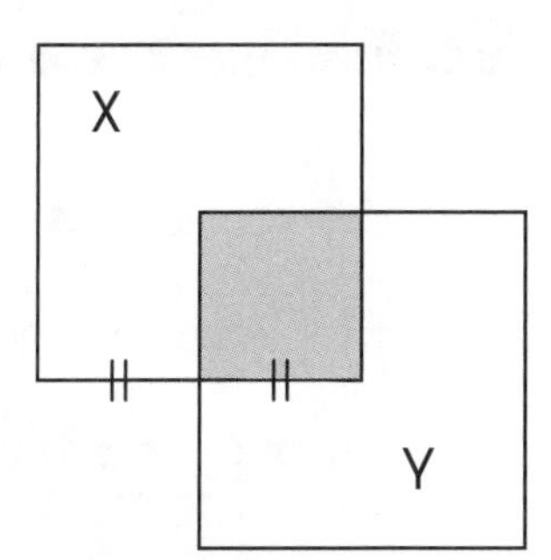

Name: ______________________ Date: ______________

Strategies

Answer the question. Express the answers as mixed numbers or fractions in simplest form.

5. A box contains six number cards. The six numbers form a pattern when ordered from least to greatest. Joanne draws these four cards from the box.

$\frac{1}{2}$	$6\frac{1}{2}$	$1\frac{1}{4}$	$\frac{1}{4}$

What number cards are likely to be left in the bag?

Solve. Express the answer in simplest form.

6. The total mass of a basket, 4 large pebbles, and 2 small pebbles is $\frac{7}{12}$ kilogram. The total mass of the basket, 2 large pebbles and 1 small pebble is $\frac{5}{12}$ kilogram. Find the mass of the empty basket.

Name: ______________________________ **Date:** ____________________

Solve. Show your work.

7. Two mystery fractions are both less than 1.

The sum of the fractions is $1\frac{1}{4}$.

The difference between the fractions is $\frac{1}{4}$.

What are the two fractions?

8. 2 plates and 3 bowls weigh $2\frac{1}{5}$ pounds.

5 plates and 6 bowls weigh $4\frac{9}{10}$ pounds.

Find the weight of one plate.

9. $\frac{2}{3}$ of Mr. Hussein's money is equal to $\frac{3}{5}$ of Ms. Lee's money. Ms. Lee has $20 more than Mr. Hussein. How much money do they have altogether?

Name: ______________________ **Date:** ______________

PROBLEM SOLVING
Exploration

Solve. Show your work.

10. Jolene and Kathy had the same number of baseball cards after Jolene gave $\frac{2}{5}$ of her cards to Kathy. They had 42 cards in all. How many baseball cards did Jolene have at first?

Show two methods for solving this problem.

Method 1

Method 2

Name: ______________________ **Date:** ______________

Solve.

11. A box contains 5 number cards. The 5 numbers form a pattern when arranged in order. Lucy draws 3 cards from the box and she places them on the table as shown.

$1\frac{3}{4}$ $1\frac{1}{2}$ 2

What two cards are likely to be left in the box? Show four different patterns.

a. 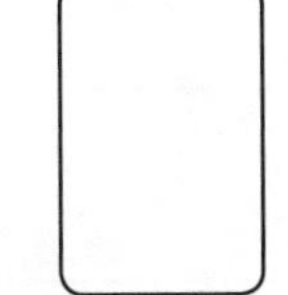 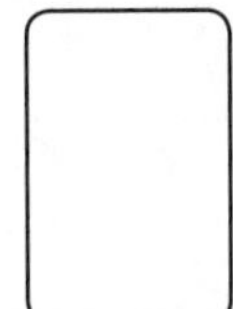 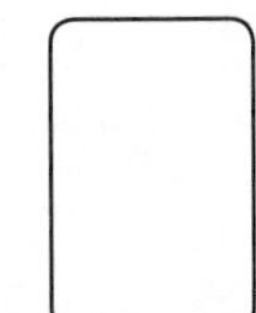 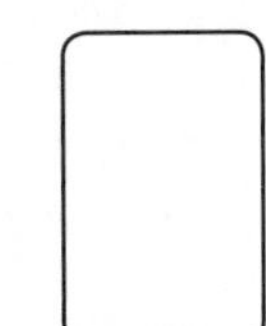 

b.    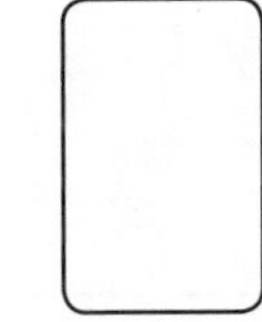 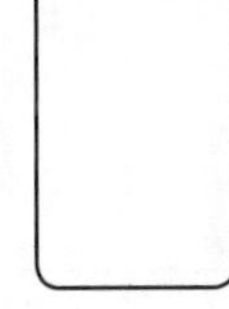

c. 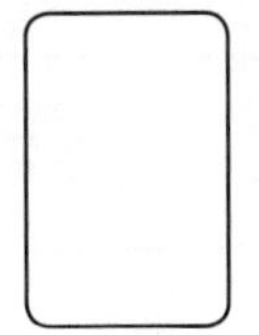 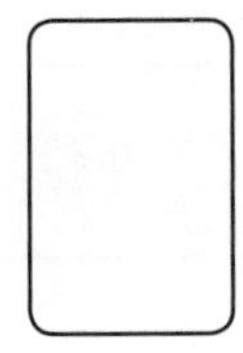  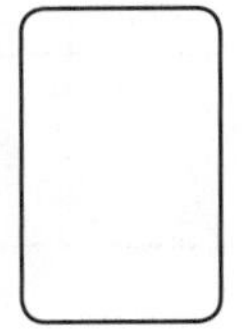 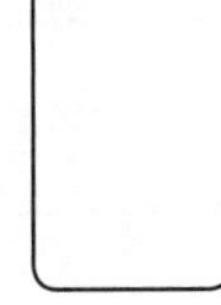

d.   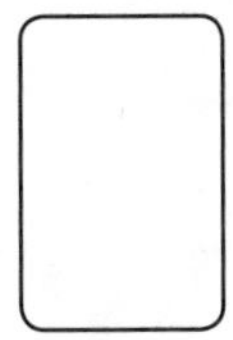 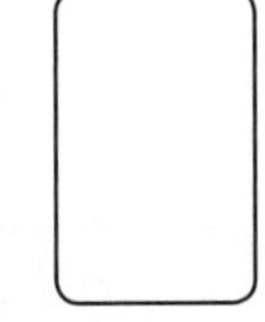 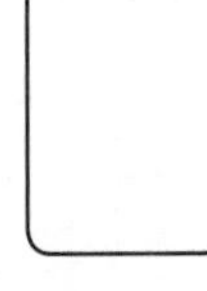

Name: ______________________ **Date:** ______________

Explain.

Jason made the following calculations. Explain the errors Jason made.

12. $\frac{1}{3} + \frac{3}{5} = \frac{4}{8}$

____

____

____

13. $\frac{9}{11} - \frac{5}{6} = \frac{4}{5}$

____

____

____

14. $\frac{2}{7} \times 21 = 21\frac{2}{7}$

____

____

____

Name: ______________________ Date: ______________

15. $1\frac{1}{2} + 3\frac{1}{4} = 4 + \frac{1}{6}$

$= 4\frac{1}{6}$

____

____

____

16.

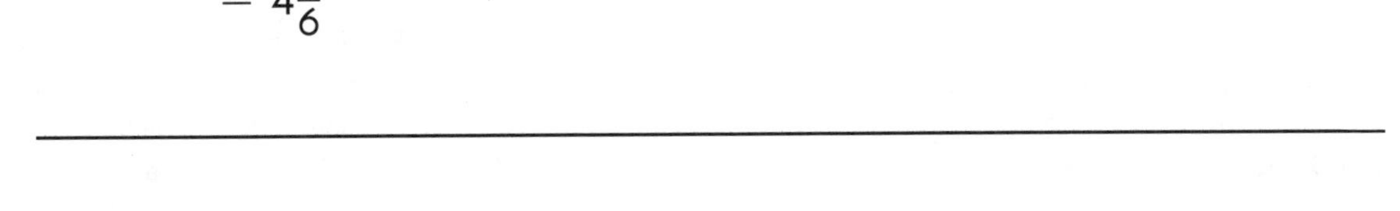

The diagram shows $\frac{3}{5}$ of a fraction strip shaded. Juliet erases some of the shading to show $\frac{3}{10}$ shaded. Explain the steps she took to shade $\frac{3}{10}$ of the fraction strip.

Step 1 ______________________________

____

Step 2 ______________________________

____

Step 3 ______________________________

____

Answers

Chapter 1

Thinking skill: Comparing

1. 78,464
2. BDAEC
   B 41,584 E 59,371
   D 56,783 C 48,745
   A 61,376
3. 94,320
   Since the greatest digit is equal to the sum of all the other four digits, then the sum has to be less than 10.
   If the digit in the ten thousands place is 8, the other digits can be 4, 3, 2, and 1.
   If the digit in the ten thousands place is 9, the other digits can be 4, 3, 2, and 0.
   The greatest possible number is 94,320.

Strategy: Look for patterns

4. 9,750; 6,000
5. 44,000
   Rule: Add 5,000 to find the next number.
6. 15,504
   All the other numbers have differences in the thousands. Also, they all end in 604.
7. There are 14 landing signal lights on each side of the runway.

1,000	3,000	5,000	7,000
1,500	3,500	5,500	7,500
2,000	4,000	6,000	
2,500	4,500	6,500	

8. 97,620
9. 20,679
10. 76,941
11. $32,012
12. 47,296 45,236 <u>43,176</u> <u>41,116</u> <u>39,056</u>
13. 2,000 should be 20,000. He used the wrong place value.
14. He used 'less than' instead of 'more than.'
15. 74,158 is greater than 63,018 but less than 82,018.
16.

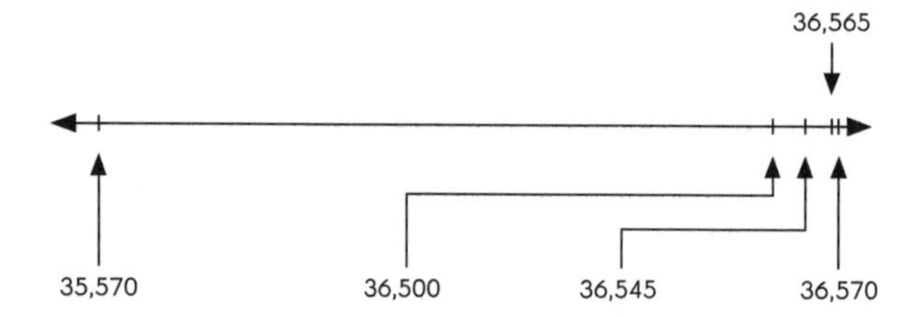

Step 1: Find the least number and place it on the left end of the number line.

Step 2: Find the greatest number and place it on the right end of the number line.

Step 3: Then place the other numbers in order between them. The value of each number in relation to other numbers determines its position on the number line.

Chapter 2

Thinking skill: Comparing

1. 25
   25 is the only factor of 50 greater than 10 and less than 40.
   1×50 2×25 5×10
2. Cost of other items (rounded to the nearest ten dollars)
   = \$20 + \$10 + \$30 = \$60
   Estimated cost of fish = \$90 − \$60 = \$30
   The least possible price of the fish is \$25.
3. The factors of 48 are 1, 2, 3, 4, 6, 8, 12, 16, 24, and 48.
   The factors of 64 are 1, 2, 4, 8, 16, 32, and 64.
   Sum (48) = $1 + 2 + 3 + 4 + 6 + 8 + 12 + 16 + 24 + 48 = 124$
   Sum (64) = $1 + 2 + 4 + 8 + 16 + 32 + 64 = 127$
   Difference = $127 - 124 = 3$
4. $x = 4$ $y = 8$
   Factors of 32: 1, 2, 4, 8, 16, and 32
   $4 + 8 = 12$
5. Strategies: Make a systematic list, Use guess and check
   Multiples of 7: 7, 14, 21, 28, 35, 42, ...
   Multiples of 4: 4, 8, 12, 16, 20, 24, 28, ...
   $4 + 18 = 22$ $8 + 18 = 26$
   $12 + 18 = 30$ $16 + 18 = 34$
   $20 + 18 = 38$ $24 + 18 = 42$
   There are 42 apples.
   $42 \div 7 = 6$ students
   There are 6 students in Ms. Duff's class.
6. Strategy: Look for patterns
   49
   All the other numbers are multiples of 3.

7. Strategies: Look for patterns, Use guess and check

Numbers	Multiples				
4 or 8	16	24	32	48	64
3	9	18	24	27	48

8. Strategies: Look for patterns, Make a systematic list
a. Sunday b. Saturday
Make a list of the days Ricky and Anwar are at the store.

First week:

Mon.	Tue.	Wed.	Thu.	Fri.	Sat.	Sun.
R	–	R	–	R	–	R
A	–	–	A	–	–	A

Second week:

Mon.	Tue.	Wed.	Thu.	Fri.	Sat.	Sun.
–	R	–	R	–	R	–
–	–	A	–	–	A	–

9.

Multiples of 9	Multiply	Divide
9	$1 \times 9 = 9$	$9 \div 1 = 9$
18	$2 \times 9 = 18$	$18 \div 2 = 9$
27	$3 \times 9 = 27$	$27 \div 3 = 9$
36	$4 \times 9 = 36$	$36 \div 4 = 9$
45	$5 \times 9 = 45$	$45 \div 5 = 9$
54	$6 \times 9 = 54$	$54 \div 6 = 9$
63	$7 \times 9 = 63$	$63 \div 7 = 9$
72	$8 \times 9 = 72$	$72 \div 8 = 9$
81	$9 \times 9 = 81$	$81 \div 9 = 9$

10. Answers vary.
Sample: Multiplication and division are inverse operations, so $18 \div 2 = 9$ and $2 \times 9 = 18$.

11. The sum is 10,185 and the difference is 4,433.
Method 1 Front-end estimation:
7,000 + 2,000 = 9,000
7,000 − 2,000 = 5,000
Method 2 Rounding to the nearest 100:
7,300 + 2,900 = 10,200
7,300 − 2,900 = 4,400
Rounding numbers to the nearest 100 gives the more accurate answers.

12. a. **Method 1** Front-end estimation
Step 1: 4,728 → 4,000; 1,095 → 1,000
Step 2: 4,000 + 1,000 = 5,000
b. **Method 2** Rounding to the nearest 100
Step 1: 4,728 → 4,700; 1,095 → 1,100
Step 2: 4,700 + 1,100 = 5,800

13. a. Error: Jack rounded 247 to 300 instead of 200.
b. Error: Keith rounded 95 to 80 instead of 100.
c. Error: Lee rounded 73 to 90 instead of 60.

Chapter 3

Thinking skill: Analyzing parts and whole

1. Quotient of 480 and 8 = 60
To find which number has 60 as its fifth multiple, divide 60 by 5.
The number is $60 \div 5 = 12$.

2. 1,102 − 56 = 1,046
1,046 ÷ 9 = 116 R 2
She needs 117 bags to pack the cookies.

3. $28 \times 36 = 1{,}008$
$12 \times 73 = 876$
1,008 − 876 = 132
132 mangoes were sold.

4. Strategy: Work backward
$120 \times 5 = 600$ pens were packed.
1,000 + 600 = 1,600
Ms. Andrews had 1,600 pens at first.

5. Thinking skill: Deduction
Strategy: Make suppositions
The product of the first 2 digits is 20, so they can only be 4, 5 or 5, 4.
5 4 ? ?
4 5 ? ?
The sum of the first and last digits is 11, so the final digit is 6 or 7.
5 4 ? 6
4 5 ? 7
The sum of all the digits is 24, so
5 4 9 6
4 5 8 7
Since the number is a multiple of 6 and the difference between the last two digits is 3, the number is 5,496.

6. Strategy: Work backward
1,007; 7
The least possible divisor is 7 since the remainder is 6.
So, $143 \times 7 + 6 = 1{,}007$.

7. Strategy: Make a systematic list

Number of Birds	Number of Dogs	Number of Heads	Number of Legs	Check
11	1	12	$11 \times 2 + 1 \times 4 = 26$	No
10	2	12	$10 \times 2 + 2 \times 4 = 28$	No
9	3	12	$9 \times 2 + 3 \times 4 = 30$	Yes

9 birds and 3 dogs

8. Strategy: Make a systematic list

Number of Tables	Number of Chairs	Total	Number of Legs
1	3	4	16
2	6	8	32
3	9	12	48
4	12	16	64
5	15	20	80

Mr. Winters borrowed 15 chairs and 5 tables.

9. 8,216 ones
821 tens 6 ones
82 hundreds 16 ones
82 hundreds 1 ten 6 ones
8 thousands 216 ones
8 thousands 20 tens 16 ones
8 thousands 2 hundreds 1 ten 6 ones

10. Answers vary. Sample:
a. Mr. Jackson has $1,250. He divides his money among 5 children. How much money does each child get?
b. Each child gets $250 from Mr. Jackson. If there are 5 children, how much money does Mr. Jackson give out?

11. **Step 1:** $5 \times 5 = 25$
Step 2: $70 \times 5 = 350$
Step 3: $200 \times 5 = 1{,}000$
Step 4: $3{,}000 \times 5 = 15{,}000$
Total 16,375

12.
$$\begin{array}{r} {}^{1}3\,{}^{3}2\,{}^{2}7\,5 \\ \times \quad 5 \\ \hline 1\,6\,3\,7\,5 \end{array}$$

13. Kelvin should have written the product as 20,375. He made the mistake of writing the product of each digit and 5 as it is. He did not regroup.

14. Melvin should have written the quotient as 815. He made the mistake of dividing the 2 tens left over without adding it to 5 ones.

15. **Step 1:** Round 827 to the nearest 100. 827 is about 800 when rounded to the nearest 100.
Step 2: Round 53 to the nearest 10. 53 is about 50 when rounded to the nearest 10.
Step 3: Multiply 800 by 50.
$800 \times 50 = 40{,}000$

Chapter 4

Thinking skill: Comparing

1. Beef
2. Vegetarian
3. $100 ÷ 50 = $2
4. Thinking skill: Comparing
Price of chicken taco → $42 ÷ 42 = $1
Price of seafood taco → $66 ÷ 33 = $2
Seafood tacos are more expensive.
5. $15 + 25 = 40$

Thinking skill: Comparing

6. $25 - 8 = 17$
7. Friday
8. Thinking skill: Identifying patterns and relationships
Accept any reasonable answer.
9. Thinking skill: Comparing
12 P.M. to 1 P.M.
10. Thinking skill: Analyzing parts and whole
Answers vary. It is unlikely, because the number of trees planted after 5 hours has been well under 1,000 so far.
11.

Number of Rotten Oranges	Number of Boxes
0	40
1	50
2	**20**
3	**30**
4	**10**
5	10

12.

Rotten Oranges

Number of Rotten Oranges	0	1	2	3	4	5
Number of Boxes	40	50	20	30	10	10

13. Thinking skill: Comparing
    30 + 10 + 10 = 50
14. Thinking skill: Analyzing parts and whole
    (1 × 50) + (2 × 20) + (3 × 30) +
    (4 × 10) + (5 × 10)
    = 50 + 40 + 90 + 40 + 50 = 270
15. Strategy: Use a diagram

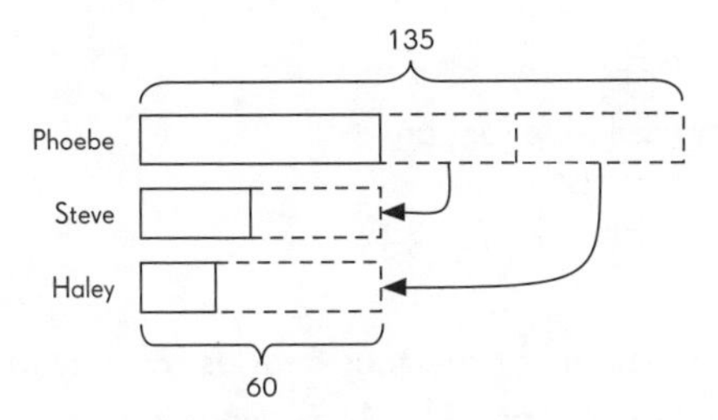

Total number of cards = 135 + 27 + 18
= 180

180 ÷ 3 = 60
60 − 18 = 42
60 − 27 = 33
Phoebe must give 42 baseball cards to Haley and 33 baseball cards to Steve so they have 60 cards each.

Strategy: Work backward

16. 24 + 15 + 23 = 62
    Justin had 62 grilled jalapenos at first.
17. Austin: 42 − 23 = 19
    Nathan: 25 − 15 = 10
    19 + 10 = 29
    Austin and Nathan had a total of 29 jalapenos at first.

Strategy: Use a diagram

18. 27 − 16 = 11
    11 more students
19. 37 + 16 = 53
    14 + 8 = 22
    53 − 22 = 31
    31 more students
20. Number of students who chose football or swimming in January = 37 + 14 = 51
    Number of students who chose football or swimming in July = 18 + 25 = 43
    51 − 43 = 8
    There was a decrease by 8 students.
21. Line graph
22. Strategy: Use a diagram
    $36 and $42

Cost of Different Lengths of Wire

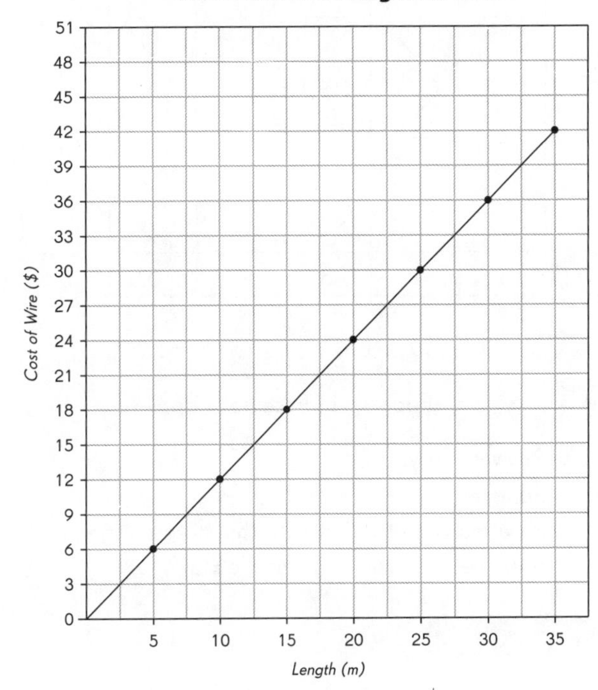

23. Answers vary. Sample reasons:
    Case 2: The temperature of the aquarium at 12 P.M. increased.
    Case 3: The temperature of the aquarium at 12 P.M. decreased.
24. **B** = 45 − 24 = 21
    C = 23 + 22 = 45
    D = 45 − 20 = 25
    E = 25 + 20 = 45
    F = 50 − 25 = 25
    G = 25 + 24 + 23 + 20 + 25 + 25
    = 142
    H = 142 + 133 = 275

25.

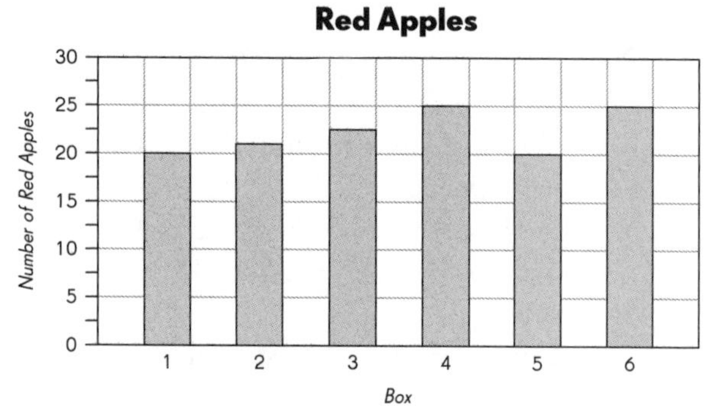

26.

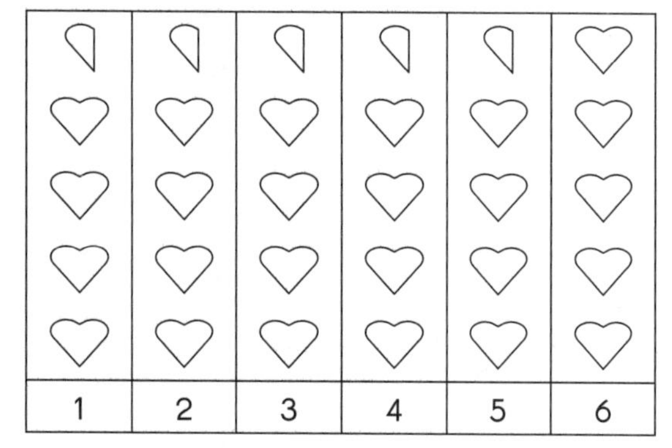

Key: Each ♡ represents 10 apples.
Each half-heart represents 5 apples.

27. Answers vary.
Sample:
How many visitors were at the store altogether over the first four hours of the day?

Chapter 5

1. Thinking skill: Analyzing parts and whole
$65 \times 4 = 260$
$69 \times 3 = 207$
$260 - 207 = 53$

2. Total possible outcomes = 3
Total number of cards = 52
Probability $= \frac{3}{52}$

3. Thinking skill: Analyzing parts and whole
$55 \times 7 = 385$
$23 + 34 + 67 + 23 + 73 + 87 = 307$
$385 - 307 = 78$

4. Thinking skill: Comparing

Flavor	Number of Students	Likelihood of High Sales
Cherry	21	more likely
Lime	9	less likely
Grape	3	less likely
Raspberry	17	more likely
Orange	0	impossible

Report: We were certain that of the 50 students surveyed, no one liked orange-flavored drinks. It is less likely that we are going to sell a lot of lime-flavored and grape-flavored drinks. Both the cherry and raspberry flavors are more likely to sell very well. It would be impossible to sell orange-flavored drinks to the students surveyed.

5. Thinking skill: Comparing
35 pounds

6. Thinking skill: Deduction
$41 \times 4 = 164$
$164 - 40 - 41 = 83$
$83 - 41 = 42$ or $83 - 42 = 41$
So, the weights of the four heaviest crates are 40 pounds, 41 pounds, 41 pounds, and 42 pounds.
Range is $42 - 19 = 23$ pounds.

7. $\frac{2}{5}$

8. Thinking skill: Comparing
White: $28 - 12 - 2 - 8 = 6$
Blue and white: $8 + 6 = 14$
Red: 12
It is more likely that Shayla will pull out a blue or white ball of yarn.

9. Strategy: Solve part of the problem
The median is 18.
____ ____ 18 ____ ____
The range is 42 and the least number is 6.
$6 + 42 = 48$ (greatest number)
6 ____ 18 ____ 48
The second greatest number is 36.
6 ____ 18 36 48
The mean is 24.
$24 \times 5 = 120$
$120 - 6 - 18 - 36 - 48$
$= 12$
6, 12, 18, 36, 48

10. Strategy: Make a systematic list
    11 ways
    a. The median is 4.
    b. For the average of four numbers to be greater than this median, their total must be greater than 16.

1st number	2nd number	3rd number	4th number	Total	Average greater than 4?
7	6	5	4	22	Yes
7	6	5	3	21	Yes
7	6	5	2	20	Yes
7	6	5	1	19	Yes
7	6	4	3	20	Yes
7	6	4	2	19	Yes
7	6	4	1	18	Yes
7	6	3	2	18	Yes
7	6	3	1	17	Yes
6	5	4	3	18	Yes
6	5	4	2	17	Yes
7	6	2	1	16	No

11. Answers vary. Possible answers:
    a. Put 2 red balls and 2 green balls in each bag.
    b. Put all red balls in each bag.
    c. Put all green balls in each bag.
    d. Put 1 red ball and 2 green balls in each bag.
    e. Put 2 red balls and 1 green ball in each bag.
12. Order of colors may vary.
    4 green, 9 blue, 3 yellow;
    5 green, 8 blue, 3 yellow;
    6 green, 7 blue, 3 yellow
13. Answers vary. Sample problem:
    Boris took 4 tests. His scores were 57, 70, 56, and 77. Find the mean of all 4 tests.
14. Answers vary. Sample problem:
    A club collected \$183, \$257, \$269, \$350, \$410, \$436, and \$475 from seven fund-raising programs. The club held another fund-raiser and had an average collection of \$312 for all programs. How much money did the club raise in the last program?
15. a. Multiply each number on the cube by the number of times it occurred. Then add all the products and divide the sum by the total number of times the cube was tossed.
    b. Find the middle number of the set of data. In this case, the middle number is 3.
    c. Find the number on the cube that occurred the most number of times. In this case, the mode is 3.

Chapter 6

1. Thinking skills: Identifying patterns and relationships, Spatial visualization
   $\frac{1}{4}$
2. Thinking skill: Comparing
   a. $\frac{7}{15}$ b. $\frac{1}{2}$
3. Thinking skill: Analyzing parts and whole
   $4\frac{2}{3} = 4\frac{6}{9}$
   $\frac{6}{9}$ liter → 3 cups
   4 liters $= \frac{36}{9}$ → 18 cups
   Total = 21 cups
   Raj used 21 cups.
4. Thinking skills: Analyzing parts and whole, Spatial visualization
   If each square is subdivided into 4 equal parts, then
   Not shaded = 6 parts
   Shaded = 1 part
   Total parts = 7 parts
   $\frac{6}{7}$ of the figure is not shaded.
5. Strategies: Look for patterns, Make a supposition
   $2\frac{1}{2}$; $4\frac{1}{4}$
   Change the numbers to like fractions:
   $\frac{2}{4}$ $\frac{26}{4}$ $\frac{5}{4}$ $\frac{1}{4}$
   Re-order the like fractions in a possible pattern:
   $\frac{1}{4} \xrightarrow{+1} \frac{2}{4} \xrightarrow{+3} \frac{5}{4}$ ____ ____ $\frac{26}{4}$
   This suggests that the subsequent 'differences' in the patterns are
   $\frac{1}{4}, \xrightarrow{+1} \frac{2}{4}, \xrightarrow{+3} \frac{5}{4}, \xrightarrow{(+5)}$?, $\xrightarrow{(+7)}$?, $\xrightarrow{(+9)} \frac{26}{4}$
   So, the two missing terms are $\frac{10}{4}$ or $2\frac{1}{2}$, and $\frac{17}{4}$ or $4\frac{1}{4}$.

6. Strategy: Simplify the problem

$\frac{7}{12} - \frac{5}{12} = \frac{2}{12}$

2 large pebbles + 1 small pebble → $\frac{2}{12}$

4 large pebbles + 2 small pebbles → $\frac{4}{12}$

So, mass of empty basket = Total mass of basket and pebbles − mass of pebbles

$\frac{7}{12} - \frac{4}{12} = \frac{3}{12} = \frac{1}{4}$

7. Strategies: Guess and check, Make suppositions

Fraction A	Fraction B	Sum $= 1\frac{1}{4}$	Difference $= \frac{1}{4}$	Answer
$\frac{1}{4}$	$\frac{1}{4}$	No	No	Wrong
$\frac{1}{4}$	$\frac{3}{4}$	No	No	Wrong
$\frac{1}{2}$	$\frac{3}{4}$	Yes	Yes	Correct

The two fractions are $\frac{3}{4}$ and $\frac{1}{2}$.

8. Strategy: Simplify the problem

Weight of 2 plates and 3 bowls → $2\frac{2}{10}$ lb

Weight of 3 plates and 3 bowls → $4\frac{9}{10} - 2\frac{2}{10}$

$= 2\frac{7}{10}$ lb

So, weight of 1 plate $= 2\frac{7}{10} - 2\frac{2}{10} = \frac{5}{10}$

$= \frac{1}{2}$ lb.

9. Strategy: Use a diagram

Mr. Hussein | $20 | ?
Ms. Lee

1 unit of Mr. Hussein's money is the same as $1\frac{1}{2}$ units of Ms. Lee's money.

$\frac{1}{2}$ unit of Ms. Lee's money → \$20

So, Ms. Lee has \$20 × 10 = \$200.
Mr. Hussein has \$200 − \$20 = \$180.
Total = \$200 + \$180
= \$380

10. **Method 1**

Jolene
Kathy

6 units → 42
1 unit → 7
5 units → 35

Method 2

At the end, each girl had $\frac{42}{2} = 21$ cards.

Jolene had 3 parts since she gave away 2 parts.

So, 1 part $= \frac{21}{3} = 7$ cards.

7 × 5 = 35
(Accept any other logical methods.)
Jolene had 35 cards at first.

11. a. $1\frac{1}{2}$ $1\frac{3}{4}$ 2 $2\frac{1}{4}$ $2\frac{1}{2}$

b. 1 $1\frac{1}{4}$ $1\frac{1}{2}$ $1\frac{3}{4}$ 2

c. $1\frac{1}{4}$ $1\frac{1}{2}$ $1\frac{3}{4}$ 2 $2\frac{1}{4}$

d. $1\frac{1}{2}$ $1\frac{5}{8}$ $1\frac{3}{4}$ $1\frac{7}{8}$ 2

12. Jason added the numerators and the denominators. He should have found a common denominator of 15 before adding the numerators.

13. Jason subtracted the numerators and the denominators. He should have found a common denominator of 66 before subtracting the numerators.

14. Jason added the fraction and the whole number, instead of finding $\frac{2}{7}$ of 21.

15. Jason added the unit fractions without finding the common denominator.

16.

Step 1: Divide the fraction strip into 10 parts.

Step 2: Convert $\frac{3}{5}$ into a fraction with a denominator of 10. $\frac{3}{5} = \frac{6}{10}$

Step 3: $\frac{6}{10} - \frac{3}{10} = \frac{3}{10}$.

Erase half the shaded area.